Chants Old & New

*A Treasury of Anglican Psalmody
Compiled by
Anthony Crossland*

Kevin Mayhew

We hope you enjoy the music in *Chants Old and New*.
Further copies are available from your local music shop or Christian bookshop.

In case of difficulty, please contact the publisher direct by writing to:

The Sales Department
KEVIN MAYHEW LTD
Rattlesden
Bury St Edmunds
Suffolk
IP30 0SZ

Phone 0449 737978
Fax 0449 737834

Please ask for our complete catalogue of outstanding Church Music.

Front Cover: *A Carol* by Edward Reginald Frampton (1872-1923)
Reproduced by kind permission of Bonhams, London/
Bridgeman Art Library, London.
Cover design by Juliette Clarke and Graham Johnstone
Picture Research: Jane Rayson

First published in Great Britain in 1994 by Kevin Mayhew Ltd

© Copyright 1994 Kevin Mayhew Ltd

ISBN 0 86209 482 8

The music in this book is protected by copyright and may not be reproduced
in any way for sale or private use without the consent of the copyright owner.

Music Editor: Donald Thomson
Music Setting: Louise Hill

Printed and bound in Great Britain

Foreword

The acquisition of Anglican chants is for me, and I suspect for many other church musicians, a personal hobby somewhat akin to stamp collecting. The core of this collection is the body of chants in regular use at Wells Cathedral, to which have been added a number of excellent chants through trade and exchange. I am extremely grateful to many of my colleagues either for having composed them or for having brought them to my attention.

As chants move from one collection to another, changes inevitably occur, and so none of the chants in this book pretends to be a definitive version. Indeed in some cases it is doubtful if such a thing exists. After considerable thought I decided that individual chants should not be allotted to specific psalms or portions thereof, this process being better left to the personal taste of the user.

I hope that the triple chants may enjoy increasing popularity. Their use is desirable, if not essential, to give coherence to such psalms as 2, 96, 137 and 146 and with a little judicious amendation they can be successfully used for others, in particular psalm 136 which has for so long suffered the verbal distortions imposed upon it by C H Lloyd's chant. Within each broad category of single, double, triple and quadruple chants items appear in alphabetical order of composer and key.

ANTHONY CROSSLAND

ANTHONY CROSSLAND (*b*.1931) studied the organ with Robert Ashfield and Malcolm Boyle. He is Organist and Master of the Choristers at Wells Cathedral and was President of the Cathedral Organist's Society from 1983 to 1985. He conducts the Wells Cathedral Oratorio Society and is also the founder and conductor of the Wells Sinfonietta.

About the Composers

The relevant chants are indicated in bold type at the end of each biography.

Walter Allcock (1861-1947) Organist at Westminster Abbey and Salisbury Cathedral. Also Organist and Composer to the Chapel Royal. **12-13**

Malcolm Archer (*b.*1952) Formerly Organist and Master of the Choristers at Bristol Cathedral, he is a recitalist, composer and conductor. **15-17**

Thomas Armstrong (*b.*1898) Organist at Exeter Cathedral and Christ Church Cathedral, Oxford. Principal of the Royal Academy of Music. **18**

Peter Aston (*b.*1938) Formerly Senior Lecturer at the University of York. Currently Professor of Music, University of East Anglia. **19**

Ivor Atkins (1869-1953) Organist at Truro, Hereford and Worcester Cathedrals. **20-23**

Thomas Attwood (1765-1838) Educated at the Chapel Royal and also studied music abroad. Organist at St Paul's Cathedral and Composer to the Chapel Royal. **24-27**

Edward Bairstow (1874-1946) Organist at Westminster Abbey and York Minster. **28-33**

Joseph Barnby (1838-1896) Precentor of Eton College and Principal of the Guildhall School of Music. **34-41**

Jonathan Battishill (1738-1801) Conductor and harpsichordist at Covent Garden Theatre and Organist at three City churches. He gave up composition after his wife ran away with an actor. **2**

William Beale (1784-1854) Gentleman of the Chapel Royal and Organist at Trinity and St John's Colleges, Cambridge. **42**

John Booth (1828-1879) Organist at St Alban's Abbey. **43**

Willam Boyce (1710-1779) A pupil of Maurice Greene, he became Organist to the Earl of Oxford's Chapel, Composer to the Chapel Royal and Master of the King's Musick. **44**

Herbert Brewer (1865-1928) An Organ Scholar at Oxford University, he held positions at Bristol and Gloucester Cathedrals. **45**

Frederick Bridge (1844-1924) Organist at Manchester Cathedral who later succeeded James Turle at Westminster Abbey. **46-47**

Percy Buck (1871-1947) Organist at Wells and Bristol Cathedrals, Director of Music at Harrow School and Professor of Music at the Universities of London and Dublin. **49-50**

Zechariah Buck (1798-1879) Organist at Norwich Cathedral. A notable trainer of boys' voices, he would fortify his choristers with a glass of port before an important solo. **51**

John Calkin (1827-1905) Organist who held various posts in Ireland and London; also Professor at the Guildhall School of Music and Trinity College of Music. **52**

Matthew Camidge (1758-1844) Chorister at the Chapel Royal who succeeded his father as Organist at York Minster. **53-54**

Edmund Chipp (1823-1886) A Chorister at the Chapel Royal, he held Organist's posts at various London churches and at Ely Cathedral. **55**

Richard Clark (1780-1856) A Gentleman of the Chapel Royal who held various positions at St George's Chapel, Windsor, Westminster Abbey and St Paul's Cathedral. **56**

Gerard Cobb (1838-1904) Fellow and Junior Bursar of Trinity College, Cambridge. President of the University Board of Musical Studies. **57**

Langdon Colborne (1835-1889) Held several significant Organist's posts including Hereford Cathedral. **58**

Marmaduke Conway (1885-1961) Organist of Wells, Chichester and Ely Cathedrals. **59**

Benjamin Cooke (1734-1793) Appointed Deputy Organist at Westminster Abbey at the age of twelve and went on to become Master of the Choristers. **60**

Robert Cooke (1768-1814) Son of Benjamin Cooke, he was also Organist at Westminster Abbey. As the result of a love affair he drowned himself in the Thames. **61**

David Cooper (*b.*1949) Was an Organ Scholar at Oxford University, and is currently Organist at Blackburn Cathedral. **3, 62-65**

George Cooper (1820-1876) Organist at various London churches and for a time Assistant Organist at St Paul's Cathedral. **66-67**

Anthony Crossland (*b.*1931) Formerly Assistant Organist at Christ Church Cathedral Oxford, he is currently Organist of Wells Cathedral. **69**

William Crotch (1775-1847) A child prodigy who was giving daily organ recitals in London at the age of four, he later became Principal of the Royal Academy of Music. It is said that he was remarkably ambidextrous and could write down the notes of two separate staves of music simultaneously. **70-72**

Harold Darke (1888-1976) Distinguished composer, teacher and organist who studied at the Royal College of Music with Parratt and Stanford. **240**

Henry Walford Davies (1869-1941) His many acheivements include Organist at St George's Chapel, Windsor and Master of the King's Musick. A prolific composer and a significant musical educator, especially through his many broadcast talks and lectures. **73-76**

Leopold Dix (1861-1935) A Dublin solicitor and amateur musician. **241**

George Dyson (1883-1964) Director of the Royal College of Music, he also held positions as Director of Music at several major public schools. **80**

Edward Elgar (1857-1934) The son of a Worcester organist and music-seller, he was virtually self-taught in composition. One of Britain's greatest composers. **81**

George Elvey (1816-1893) Organist at St George's Chapel, Windsor and Private Organist to Queen Victoria. **82-86**

Stephen Elvey (1805-1860) Brother of the above. He lost his right leg in a shooting accident but with a wooden substitute became an accomplished organist. **87**

Gerald Finzi (1901-1956) Taught at the Royal Academy of Music and was particularly distinguished as a song-writer, although his music is not widely known. **88-89**

Luke Flintoft (*d.*1727) Minor Canon of Westminster Abbey. **90**

George Garrett (1834-1897) Organist at Madras Cathedral, St John's College, Cambridge and also University Organist. **91-94**

Henry Gauntlett (1805-1876) Organist at St Bartholomew-the-Less Church, London. **95**

Francis Gladstone (1845-1928) A pupil of Samuel Sebastian Wesley, his acheivements included Organist at Norwich Cathedral and Professor of Harmony and Counterpoint at the Royal College of Music. **96**

John Goss (1800-1880) Began his career as a singer but soon decided to become a church musician. One of his best-known anthems, *If we believe*, was composed for the funeral of the Duke of Wellington. **97-107**

George Guest (*b.*1924) Organist at Chester Cathedral and St John's College, Cambridge. Appointed University Organist in 1974. **108**

William Harris (1883-1973) Organist whose appointments included Lichfield Cathedral, Christ Church Cathedral, Oxford and St George's Chapel, Windsor. **110**

Harry Hast (1862-1944) A professional tenor singer, who was formerly a member of the choir at Westminster Abbey. Upon retiring he taught at the Guildhall School of Music. **111**

Henry McLeod Havergal (*b.*1902) Director of Music at several major public schools before his appointment as Principal of the Royal Scottish Academy of Music. **242**

William Henry Havergal (1793-1870) Honorary Canon of Worcester Cathedral. **112-113**

Edward Higgins (*d.*1769) Organist at Bristol Cathedral and Lay Vicar Choral of Christ Church and St Patrick's Cathedrals, Dublin. **116**

Henry Hiles (1826-1904) English organist, composer and teacher who helped to promote the Incorporated Society of Musicians. **4**

Alfred Hollins (1865-1942) Blind from birth, he established himself firstly as a concert pianist then as an organ recitalist, touring the British Empire and the USA. **117**

Edward Hopkins (1818-1901) Organist at the Temple Church, he was an authority on church organ design and construction. **118-123**

John Hopkins (1820-1873) Cousin of the above. Organist at Rochester Cathedral, Trinity College, Cambridge and University Organist. **124**

Herbert Howells (1892-1983) A pupil of Herbert Brewer, he was a distinguished composer, both of church and secular music, and was greatly involved with the Three Choirs' Festival. **126-128**

John Hughes (*d.*1934) Organist at Chester Cathedral. **129**

Haydn Keeton (1847-1921) Organist at Peterborough Cathedral. **130, 243**

Gerald Knight (1908-1979) Organist at Canterbury Cathedral, he was later appointed Director of the Royal School of Church Music. **131**

Richard Latham (1906-1980) London Organist and Professor at the Royal College of Music. **133**

William Lawes (*c.*1602-1645) Musician 'in ordinary for the lute and voices' at the court of Charles I. He fought in the Civil War and was killed during the siege of Chester. **134-135**

Charles Lavington (1819-1895) A pupil of James Turle at Westminster Abbey, he later became Organist at Wells Cathedral. **136**

Henry Ley (1887-1964) Organist at Christ Church Cathedral, Oxford and also held the position of Precentor and Director of Music at Eton College. **137-140, 244**

Charles Lloyd (1849-1919) Organist at Gloucester Cathedral, Christ Church Cathedral, Oxford and Precentor and Organist at Eton College. **141-142**

Henry Longhurst (1819-1904) Organist at Canterbury Cathedral. His father added seven 16ft pedal pipes to the organ and William related that, as a six-year old, he was made to crawl inside one of these and sing. Few Cathedral Organists can say that they have sung a solo from inside one of their own organ pipes. **143**

Martin Luther (1483-1546) The noted German theologian and reformer. This chant is adapted from his hymn-tune *Ein' feste Burg*. **144**

Henry Mann (1850-1929) Organist at King's College, Cambridge, who transformed the choir into one of the foremost of Anglican choirs, persuading the College authorities to establish a choir school and replace the lay clerks with choral scholars. **145**

Stanley Marchant (1883-1949) Organist at St Paul's Cathedral and Professor of Music at London University. **146**

Phillip Marshall (*b.*1921) Organist at Ripon and Lincoln Cathedrals. **147-148**

George Martin (1844-1916) Succeeded John Stainer as Master of the Choristers and Organist at St Paul's Cathedral. **149**

Richard Massey (1798-1893) Organist at the Chapel Royal, Whitehall. **150-151**

Samuel Matthews (1769-1832) Organist at Trinity and St John's Colleges, Cambridge. **152**

Charles Miller (1856-1933) A solicitor by profession, he was also Organist at two London churches. **153**

Edwin Monk (1819-1900) Organist at York Minster, he was a keen astronomer and a Fellow of the Royal Astronomical Society. **154-155**

Wilfrid Mothersole (1898-1992) Assistant Organist and a member of the choir at St Edmundsbury Cathedral. **156**

Herbert Murrill (1909-1952) Professor of Composition at the Royal Academy of Music and Head of Music at the BBC. He wrote a small quantity of church music and some secular compositions including a string quartet and two cello concertos. **157**

James Nares (1715-1783) Held several positions including Organist at York Minster at the age of nineteen. The retiring organist was indignant that 'a child' should succeed him, so in his first days at York, Nares faultlessly transposed a particularly difficult service down a semitone to show his predecessor what a child could do. **158**

Michael Nicholas (*b*.1938) Organist at Norwich Cathedral. **5-6**

June Nixon Organist and Director of the Choir at St Paul's Cathedral, Melbourne, Australia. She also teaches at the Melbourne University School of Music. **159-164**

Thomas Noble (1867-1953) Organist at Trinity College, Cambridge, Ely Cathedral and York Minster. He then pursued a distinguished musical career in the USA. **165-168**

Herbert Oakeley (1830-1903) Professor of Music at Edinburgh University, he wrote mainly choral music. **169, 246**

Frederick Ouseley (1825-1889) A great figure in the revival of English church music during the nineteenth century. Founder of St Michael's College, Tenbury, Professor of Music at Oxford University and Precentor of Hereford Cathedral. **170-171**

Walter Parratt (1841-1924) Organist at St George's Chapel, Windsor, and Professor of Music at Oxford University. **174**

Hubert Parry (1848-1918) English composer, teacher and writer, he began composing at the age of eight and took a music degree whilst still a schoolboy at Eton. Director of the Royal College of Music and Professor of Music at Oxford University. **175-176**

John Pratt (1772-1855) Organist at King's College, Cambridge and Cambridge University Organist. **177**

Henry Purcell (1659-1695) Composer-in-ordinary for the violins to Charles II and Organist of Westminster Abbey and the Chapel Royal. The greatest English composer of the seventeenth century. **178**

Kellow Pye (1812-1901) Composer and pianist. **179-180**

John Randall (1715-1799) Organist at King's and Trinity Colleges, Cambridge, and Professor of Music, Cambridge University. **181**

William Russell (1777-1813) Organist at the Foundling Hospital, London. **182**

Andrew Seivewright (*b*.1926) Organist at Carlisle Cathedral and Lecturer at Edinburgh and Glasgow Universities. **7, 183-184**

Henry Smart (1813-1879) Pursued an active career as an organist and composer despite being blind for the last fifteen years of his life. **185-188**

John Soaper (1743-1794) Composer and singer. **189**

Charles South (1850-1916) Organist at Salisbury Cathedral. **190**

John Stainer (1840-1901) A notable choir-trainer, musical historian and educator. He held several Organist's posts and was Professor of Music at Oxford University. **191-194**

Charles Stanford (1852-1924) A gifted composer and teacher, he was Professor of Composition at the Royal College of Music and Professor of Music at Cambridge University. **195-197**

Heathcote Statham (1889-1973) Organist whose appointments included Calcutta and Norwich Cathedrals. **8**

Charles Steggall (1826-1905) London organist and composer of church music. **9**

Robert Stewart (1825-1894) Organist at Christ Church Cathedral, Dublin and Professor of Music at Dublin University. **198**

Charles Hylton Stewart (1884-1932) Organist at King's College, Cambridge, Chester and Rochester Cathedrals and St George's Chapel, Windsor. **199-201**

Henry Stonex (1823-1897) Organist at Norwich Cathedral. **203**

James Taylor (*b.*1833) Organist at New College, Oxford. **205**

Thomas Tomkins (1572-1656) A pupil of William Byrd, he was Organist at Worcester Cathedral and Organist and Gentleman of the Chapel Royal. **10**

James Turle (1802-1882) Organist at Westminster Abbey. His personal recipe for choristers faced with an important solo was a glass of sherry with an egg beaten into it. **207-212**

Stanley Vann (*b.*1910) Successively Organist at Chelmsford and Peterborough Cathedrals. He is a composer, conductor and teacher of singing. **213-216**

Frederick Wadeley (1882-1970) Organist at Malvern Priory Church and Carlisle Cathedral. **217-221**

Thomas Attwood Walmisley (1814-1856) Composer and organist, he was the godson of Thomas Attwood, who instructed him in harmony. **224-230**

Samuel Wesley (1766-1837) A child prodigy who composed an oratorio at the age of eight. One of the foremost organists, conductors, composers and lecturers of his day. **231-232**

Samuel Sebastian Wesley (1810-1876) Son of the above. The greatest figure in nineteenth century English church music, he was Organist at Hereford, Exeter, Winchester and Gloucester Cathedrals. **233-236**

Percy Whitlock (1903-1946) A distinguished composer of church and organ music, he held posts at Rochester and Bournemouth. **237, 245**

Charles Wood (1866-1926) Studied with Stanford whom he later succeeded as Professor of Music at Cambridge. **238**

Richard Woodward (1744-1777) Organist at Christ Church Cathedral and Master of the Choristers at Christ Church and St Patrick's Cathedrals, Dublin. **239**

SINGLE CHANTS

1 Anon

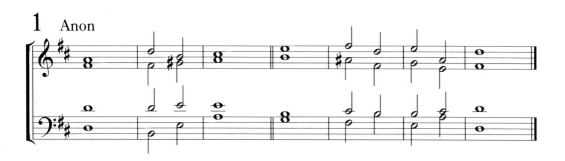

2 Jonathan Battishill

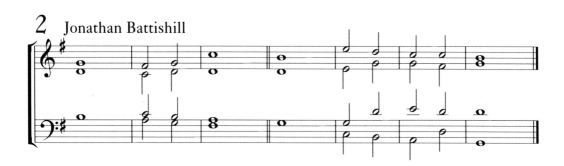

3 David Cooper

4 Henry Hiles

5 Michael Nicholas

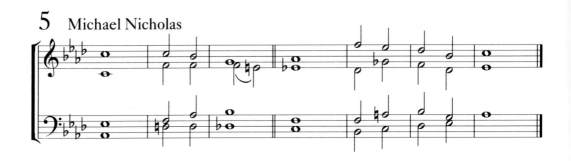

6 Michael Nicholas

7 Andrew Seivewright

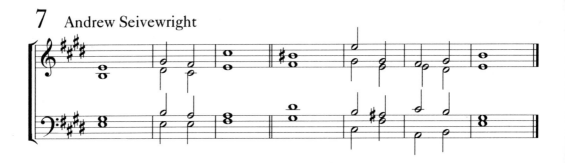

8 Heathcote Statham

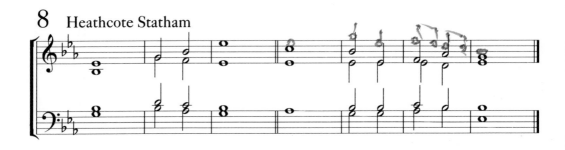

9 Charles Steggall

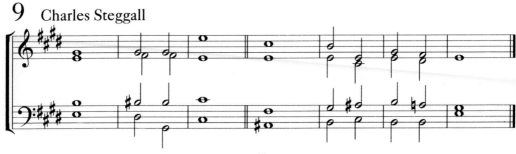

10 Thomas Tomkins

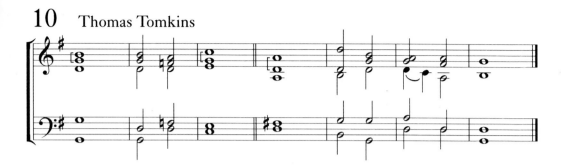

11 Thomas Attwood Walmisley

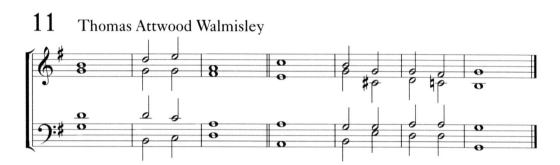

DOUBLE CHANTS

12 Walter Alcock

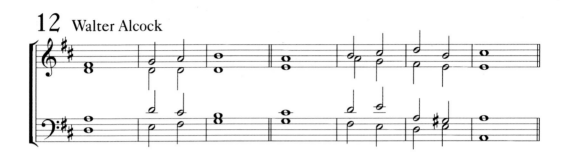

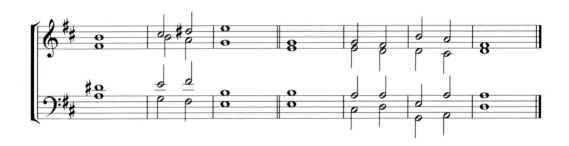

13 Walter Alcock

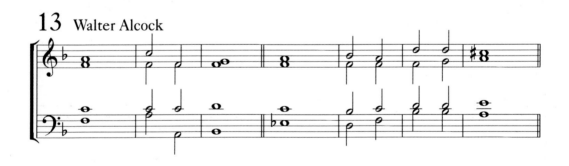

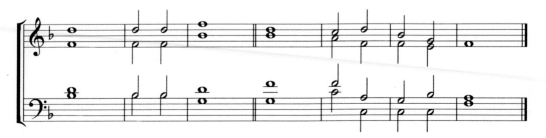

14 Terence Allbright

15 Malcolm Archer

16 Malcolm Archer

17 Malcolm Archer

18 Thomas Armstrong

19 Peter Aston

26 Thomas Attwood

27 Thomas Attwood

28 Edward Bairstow

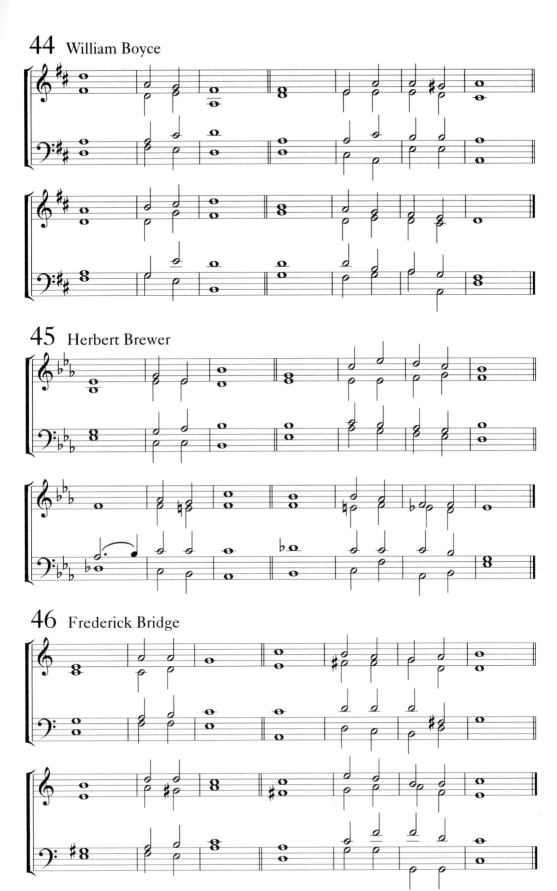

56 Richard Clark

57 Gerard Cobb

58 Langdon Colborne

59 Marmaduke Conway

60 Benjamin Cooke

61 Robert Cooke

71 William Crotch

72 William Crotch

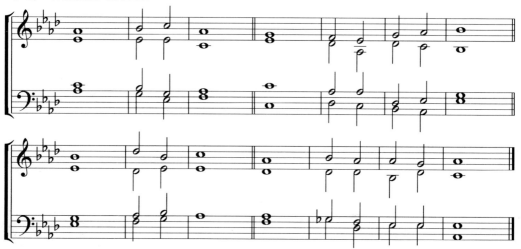

73 Henry Walford Davies

80 George Dyson

81 Edward Elgar

82 George Elvey

95 Henry Gauntlett

96 Francis Gladstone

97 John Goss

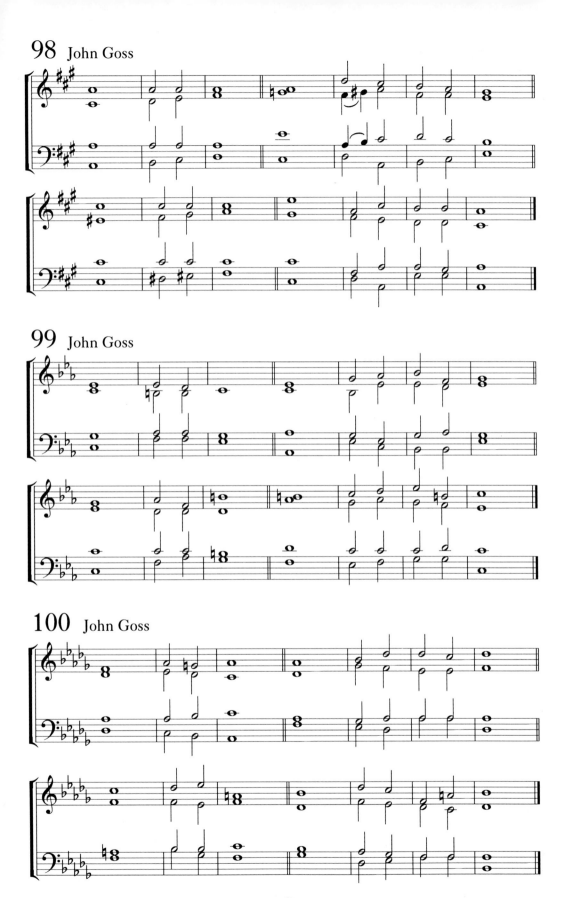

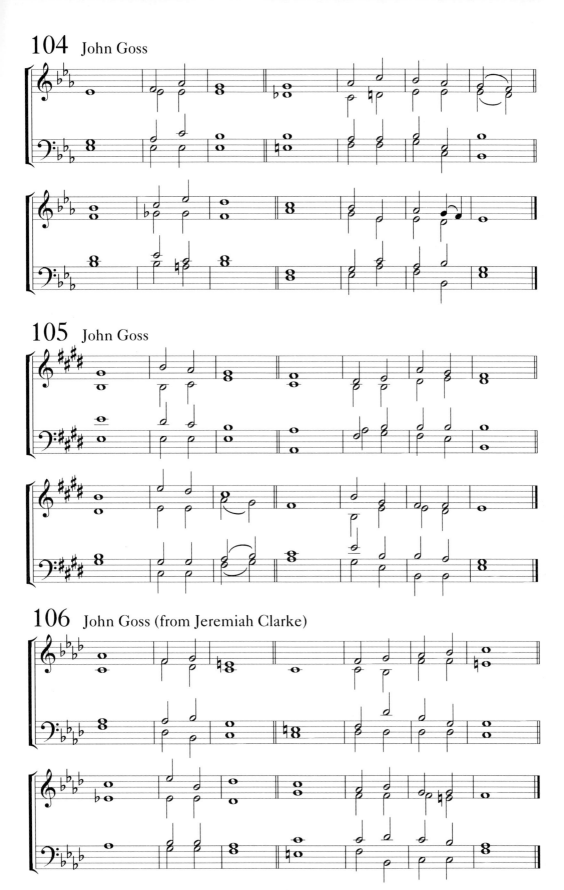

113 William Havergal

114 F. J. A. Hervey

115 F. J. A. Hervey

116 Edward Higgins

117 Alfred Hollins

118 Edward Hopkins

119 Edward Hopkins

120 Edward Hopkins

121 Edward Hopkins

122 Edward Hopkins

123 Edward Hopkins

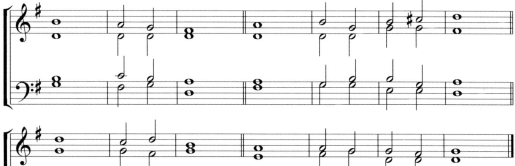
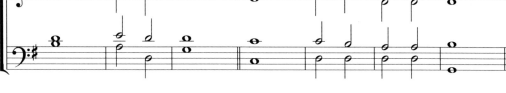

124 John Hopkins

125 Martin How

126 Herbert Howells

127 Herbert Howells

131 Gerald Knight

132 Lambie

133 Richard Latham

134 William Lawes

135 William Lawes

136 Charles Lavington

149 George Martin

150 Richard Massey

151 Richard Massey

155 Edwin Monk

156 Wilfrid Mothersole

157 Herbert Murrill

161 June Nixon

162 June Nixon

163 June Nixon

164 June Nixon

165 Thomas Noble

166 Thomas Noble

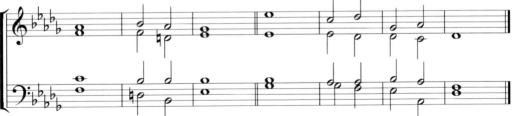

170 Frederick Ouseley

171 Frederick Ouseley

172 Parr (arr. Anthony Crossland)

191 John Stainer

192 John Stainer

193 John Stainer (arr. Anthony Crossland)

221 Frederick Wadely

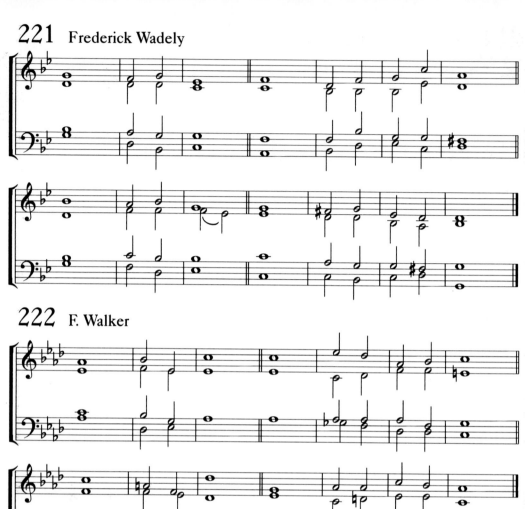

222 F. Walker

223 Robert Walker

224 Thomas Attwood Walmisley

225 Thomas Attwood Walmisley

226 Thomas Attwood Walmisley

227 Thomas Attwood Walmisley

228 Thomas Attwood Walmisley

229 Thomas Attwood Walmisley

230 Thomas Attwood Walmisley

231 Samuel Wesley

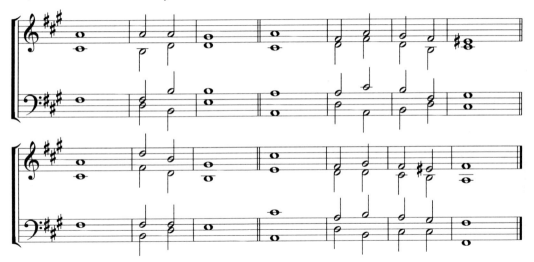

232 Samuel Wesley

239 Richard Woodward

TRIPLE CHANTS

240 Harold Darke

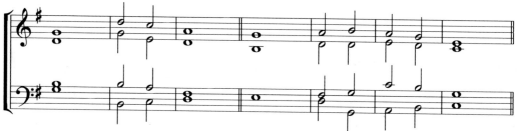

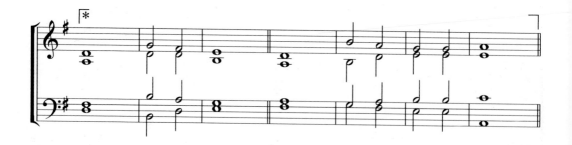

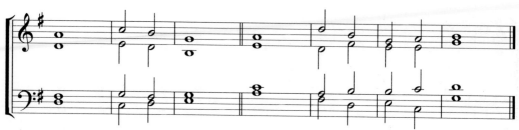

* Omit these bars in Gloria

241 Leopold Dix

242 Henry Havergal

* Omit these bars in Gloria

243 Haydn Keeton

244 Henry Ley

* Omit these bars in Gloria

245 Percy Whitlock

* Omit these bars in Gloria

QUADRUPLE CHANT

246 Herbert Oakeley

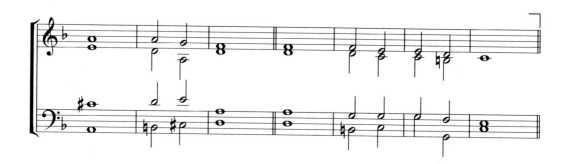

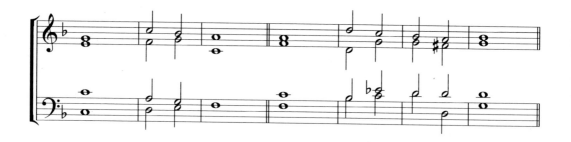

* Omit these bars in Gloria

Index of Keys

Key	Chant	Page	Composer
SINGLE CHANTS			
A♭ major	4	9	Hiles
	5	10	Nicholas
C major	6	10	Nicholas
D major	1	9	Anon
E♭ major	3	9	Cooper
	8	10	Statham
E major	7	10	Seivewright
	9	10	Steggall
G major	2	9	Battishill
	10	11	Tomkins
	11	11	Walmisley
DOUBLE CHANTS			
A♭ major	24	16	Attwood
	25	16	Attwood
	43	22	Booth
	72	32	Crotch
	77	34	Day
	78	34	Day
	125	50	How
	140	55	Ley
	147	57	Marshall
	195	73	Stanford
	217	80	Wadeley
	222	82	F Walker
	224	83	Walmisley
	237	87	Whitlock
	238	87	Wood
A minor	34	19	Barnby
	42	22	Beale
	56	27	Clark
	185	70	Smart
	191	72	Stainer
	204	76	Talbot
A major	15	13	Archer
	18	14	Armstrong
	20	15	Atkins
	21	15	Atkins
	35	20	Barnby
	57	27	Cobb

Key	Chant	Page	Composer
(A major cont.)	59	28	Conway
	82	35	G Elvey
	91	38	Garrett
	97	40	Goss
	98	41	Goss
	118	47	Hopkins
	149	58	Martin
	156	60	Mothersole
	159	61	Nixon
	165	63	Noble
	170	65	Ouseley
	171	65	Ouseley
	186	70	Smart
	199	74	C Stewart
	207	77	Turle
B♭ minor	126	50	Howells
B♭ major	127	50	Howells
	129	51	Hughes
	177	67	Pratt
	225	83	Walmisley
B minor	158	61	Nares
	178	67	Purcell
B major	119	48	Hopkins
	218	81	Wadeley
	226	83	Walmisley
C minor	22	15	Atkins
	79	34	Deffell
	99	41	Goss
	134	53	Lawes
	219	81	Wadeley
C major	26	17	Attwood
	46	23	Bridge
	47	24	Bridge
	73	32	Davies
	81	35	Elgar
	83	36	G Elvey
	110	45	W Harris
	120	48	Hopkins
	135	53	Lawes
	137	54	Ley
	143	56	Longhurst

Key	Chant	Page	Composer
(C major *cont.*)	144	56	Luther
	190	71	South
	200	75	C Stewart
	208	77	Turle
	213	79	Vann
	214	79	Vann
	215	80	Vann
C♯ minor	61	28	R Cooke
D♭ major	29	18	Bairstow
	100	41	Goss
	166	63	Noble
	167	64	Noble
	216	80	Vann
D minor	36	20	Barnby
	58	27	Colborne
	62	29	D Cooper
	63	29	D Cooper
	70	31	Crotch
	71	32	Crotch
	74	33	Davies
	88	37	Finzi
	101	42	Goss
	128	51	Howells
	196	73	Stanford
	209	78	Turle
	210	78	Turle
	233	86	S S Wesley
	234	86	S S Wesley
D major	12	12	Alcock
	14	13	Allbright
	30	18	Bairstow
	44	23	Boyce
	84	36	G Elvey
	102	42	Goss
	111	45	Hast
	112	45	W Havergal
	124	49	Hopkins
	132	52	Lambie
	138	54	Ley
	139	54	Ley
	141	55	Lloyd
	145	56	Mann
	148	57	Marshall

Key	Chant	Page	Composer
(D major *cont.*)	160	61	Nixon
	161	62	Nixon
	168	64	Noble
	183	69	Seivewright
	227	84	Walmisley
	239	88	Woodward
E♭ minor	169	64	Oakeley
E♭ major	16	13	Archer
	23	16	Atkins
	28	17	Bairstow
	31	18	Bairstow
	37	20	Barnby
	45	23	Brewer
	49	24	P Buck
	64	29	D Cooper
	75	33	Davies
	96	40	Gladstone
	103	42	Goss
	104	43	Goss
	109	44	T Harris
	117	47	Hollins
	150	58	Massey
	152	59	Matthews
	153	59	Miller
	162	62	Nixon
	163	62	Nixon
	174	66	Parratt
	181	68	Randall
	184	69	Seivewright
	189	71	Soaper
	202	75	Stocks
	205	76	Taylor
E minor	38	21	Barnby
	53	26	Camidge
	192	72	Stainer
	203	76	Stonex
	206	77	Teesdale
E major	17	14	Archer
	27	17	Attwood
	32	19	Bairstow
	54	26	Camidge
	55	26	Chipp
	76	33	Davies

Key	Chant	Page	Composer
(E major *cont.*)	87	37	S Elvey
	89	38	Finzi
	95	40	Gauntlett
	105	43	Goss
	108	44	Guest
	113	46	W Havergal
	130	51	Keeton
	142	55	Lloyd
	175	66	Parry
	176	67	Parry
	179	68	Pye
	182	69	Russell
	193	72	Stainer
	198	74	R Stewart
	211	78	Turle
	228	84	Walmisley
F minor	48	24	Brownsmith
	65	30	D Cooper
	85	36	G Elvey
	106	43	Goss
	115	46	Hervey
	212	79	Turle
	220	81	Wadeley
	229	84	Walmisley
F major	13	12	Alcock
	33	19	Bairstow
	39	21	Barnby
	80	35	Dyson
	86	37	G Elvey
	92	39	Garrett
	93	39	Garrett
	107	44	Goss
	116	47	Higgins
	121	48	Hopkins
	133	52	Latham
	154	59	Monk
	197	74	Stanford
	230	85	Walmisley
	235	86	S S Wesley
	236	87	S S Wesley
F♯ minor	231	85	S Wesley
F♯ major	164	63	Nixon

Key	Chant	Page	Composer
G minor	40	21	Barnby
	90	38	Flintoft
	122	49	Hopkins
	136	53	Lavington
	172	65	Parr
	221	82	Wadeley
	223	82	R Walker
G major	19	14	Aston
	41	22	Barnby
	50	25	P Buck
	51	25	Z Buck
	52	25	Calkin
	60	28	B Cooke
	66	30	G Cooper
	67	30	G Cooper
	68	31	G Cooper
	69	31	Crossland
	94	39	Garrett
	114	46	Hervey
	123	49	Hopkins
	131	52	Knight
	146	57	Marchant
	151	58	Massey
	155	60	Monk
	157	60	Murrill
	173	66	Parr
	180	68	Pye
	187	70	Smart
	188	71	Smart
	194	73	Stainer
	201	75	C Stewart
	232	85	S Wesley

TRIPLE CHANTS

Key	Chant	Page	Composer
A major	241	89	Dix
B♭ major	243	90	Keeton
C major	244	90	Ley
E minor	245	91	Whitlock
E major	242	89	H Havergal
G major	240	88	Darke

QUADRUPLE CHANT

Key	Chant	Page	Composer
F major	246	92	Oakeley

Acknowlegements

The Publishers wish to express their gratitude to the following composers and publishers for permission to use copyright material:

Chants 214 -216 by Stanley Vann are extracted from *Peterborough Chants* - a collection of thirty-three chants composed for his use with the choir of Peterborough Cathedral.
The complete collection is available from Anglo-American Music Publishers, 4 Kendall Avenue, Sanderstead, Surrey CR2 0NH by whose permission they are here reprinted.
Chants 214-216 © 1985 Anglo-American Music Publishers, London. All rights reserved.

Peter Aston for chant 19.

The Estate of Edward Bairstow for chants 28-33.

David Cooper for chants 3 and 62-65.

George Guest for chant 108.

The Estate of Richard Latham for chant 133.

The Estate of Wilfrid Mothersole for chant 156.

Michael Nicholas for chants 5-6.

Novello & Co Ltd, 8/9 Frith Street, London W1V 5TZ
for chants 12-13 by Walter Alcock, 20-33 by Ivor Atkins and 49-50 by Percy Buck.

Oxford University Press, 3 Park Road, London NW1 6XN
for chants 137-140 by Henry Ley, 146 by Stanley Marchant and 245 by Percy Whitlock.

The Royal School of Church Music, Addington Palace, Croydon, Surrey CR9 5AD
for chants 125 by Martin How and 131 by Gerald Knight.

Andrew Seivewright for chants 7 and 183-184.

Michael Statham for chant 8 by Heathcote Statham.

Robert Walker for chant 223.

The copyright of the following chants is vested in Kevin Mayhew Ltd, Rattlesden, Bury St Edmunds, Suffolk IP30 0SZ: 159-164 by June Nixon, 147-148 by Phillip Marshall and 15-17 by Malcolm Archer.

Every effort has been made to trace the owners of copyright material, and we hope that no copyright has been infringed. Pardon is sought and apology made if the contrary be the case, and a correction will be made in any reprint of this book.